# Creative Voices of Uganda

presented by Harker Shaw Poetry

poetry by the students of Busano Community, Uganda
accompanied by art from artist around the world

Creative Voices of Uganda
presented by Harker Shaw Poetry

poetry by the students of Busano Community, Uganda
accompanied by art from artist around the world

edited by Joanna Harker Shaw
Printed in the UK by lulu.com

copyright
All works remain the intellectual property of their authors
The book *Creative Voices of Uganda* is © Harker Shaw Poetry 2020, and it may not be reproduced in full or in part without consent.

ISBN - 978-1-71650-036-7

# Creative Voices of Uganda

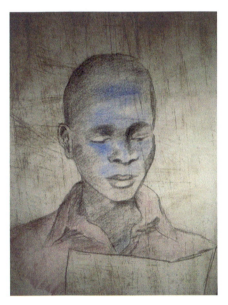

# Creative Voices of Uganda

## Busano Community

The poems in this book were all written over the summer of 2020 when the world was in lockdown to stop COVID19. Schools in Uganda closed and students were left with no academic support. Nkaaba Jude, director of the Busano Community Initiative, and Joanna Harker Shaw, lecturer in English and Creative Writing at St Mary's University, devised an online writing course to continue the students' intellectual development.
The course was delivered by Joanna teaching by video call from London, with small groups of students in Uganda gathered around one computer, and Jude on hand to provide translations when necessary.
The result was a fruitful and enjoyable experience for all involved. With no other school work the students developed wonderfully, and it was Joanna's idea to celebrate their achievements with this book.

All of the money raised will go directly back to the Busano Community, aiding them to provide more education facilities to their remarkable students.

Also by Joanna Harker Shaw

The Witches of Aira Falls Poetry Workbook
*an illustrated poetry workbook for children aged 7-12*

Songs of the River
*collected poems*

The Darkness and the Dawn
*a memoir of depression*

The Butterfly Opiate
*photographic poetry pamphlet*

Acknowledgments

I would like to express my deep gratitude to those who have assisted this book

to Nkaaba Jude for his tireless labours for these students, his assistance in the classes, and his work in collecting work from the students;

to Babirye Mary, school administrator and Executive Director for Busano Community Initiative Uganda for her support in lessons;

to Greg Harker Shaw for creating the book cover and font;

to those who have assisted with the assembling, editing, and promotion of this book, or simply with their advice:
Jax Braithwaite, Keith Buckman, Peter DeGraft Johnson (The Repeat Beat Poet), Andrew Jackson, Nicola Murnaghan, Louise Roberts, Cameron Touchard-Harding, Kieran Rayner, Breone Sanders, Ryoko Tada.

to all the board of BCUI, Nkaaba Jude and Babirye Mary as already mentioned, and alsoNkaaba Caesar, Kisoma Brenda, Kisoma Sandra, and Sebidde Alexander.

to the artists who have kindly allowed the use of their art in this book;

and of course to the students for all their hard work, and for the joy they bring me.

This book was the work of many hands.
Thank you.

Joanna Harker Shaw

Contents

Foreword by Nkaaba Jude 12

School and Education

School Life by Nangobi Bridget 18
Education by Nangobi Maria 19
Young Women of Uganda by Joanna Harker Shaw 21
Oh! The Book! by Kasadha Maliki Malson 22
Books Are Our Teachers by Alibawa Ali 23
Song of a School Boy by Katunde Abbay 24
Teaching from England by Joanna Harker Shaw 25
The Power of words by Dhikusooka Ernest and Babirye Mary 26

Nature
Land, Land by Mwesigwa Timothy 30
Valley by Kitimbo Viccent 32
In Praise of the Flowers by Nangobi Maria 34
Mountains by Kasule David 36
Protecting Our Forests by Awino Maria 37
From Seeds I Grow by Kasadha Maliki Malson 38
The Tree by Kintu Emmanuel 39
The Sun's Song by Mukisa Andrew 40

The Pearl of Africa by Dhikusooka Ernest and Babirye Mary

Our Lives
Walking with my brothers by Nakisige Dorcus
Little Mango by Alibaawa Ali
My Brother in the Mango tree by Veronica Faith
The Gift by Kintu Emmanuel
My Queen by Muwanguzi Samuel (Samuel Izon)
Street Life by Sebbide Kenneth 53
Poverty Sebbide Kenneth 54
Building the Nation by Nangobi Peace Praise 56

Accidents by Kasule Maliki Malson 58
Advice for the Children by Kintu Emmanuel 60
Good News by Kasadha Maliki Malson 61
A Mother's Song by Sebidde Kenneth 62
Sponsors by Mukisa Andrew 63
The Good of my Sister by Muwanguzi Samuel (Smauel Izon) 64

The World
Life Life Life! by Nangobi Bridget 68
Death by Mukyane Faruku 69
Time by Kintu Emmanuel 70
The Grace by Mukisa Andrew 72
Diseases by Kitamirike Deogratius 73
COVID 19 by Muwanguzi Samuel (Samuel Izon) 75
Future Without Trees by Dhikusooka Ernest 76
Fire Bird by Mukyawe Faruku

Learning in Lockdown by Joanna Harker Shaw 78

About the artists

Meet the students

## Foreword by Nkaaba Jude

Being born in the countryside has not deterred me from fulfilling my purpose in a tolerant world. I couldn't imagine that today we would have a creative masterpiece by stitching words together to fire a shot heard across the world.

Busano community initiative Uganda is committed to the long-lasting transformation of vulnerables and the empowerment of communities through education and self-sustainability. We understand that though there are differences amongst, the problems we face are shared. And with what can unite us, we hope to work together for the common goal of giving the abandoned, orphaned, disabled and disadvantaged children a decent mode of life. As a nonprofit organisation, we are committed to serve beyond the border lines of the community we live in. Despite our background, age, sex or gender we live and love to share with those who can't support themselves as we stand firm to keep the lamp of hope burning.

Our dear readers, the world has changed and we too have to changed. You will find many interesting stories of the young generation of Uganda the pearl of Africa who are striving hard to make ends meet. Such an improbable journey where the youths are involved to make their voice heard is a stepping stone to shape a future full of idealism that will mitigate the current miseries. I am hopeful that with the best team we have laid a stone and written our names in the library of fame across the globe. This is the best we could do at the moment as we keep striving for the best. Enjoy.

nkajude2@gmail.com
+256756403875
Nkaaba jude
Executive director
Busano community initiative Uganda

*Bowed heads in the classroom*
*Pens whisper across paper*
*Poetry is made*


Joanna Harker Shaw

# Creative Voices of Uganda

## POETRY

# School

## School Life is all I love

Smartly dressed in my blue uniform
My hair very neat
And my shoes shining bright
Every passerby admires
As I am on my way to school

School Life is all I love

Sharing is part of my life
My friends and I are
Cracking jokes and playing games
Keeping us fit
As we work hard
To achieve our one goal of success

School Life is all I love

New experiences every day
I am always gaining knowledge
By solving problems mathematical
Reading stories
Reciting poems

Yes, School Life is all I love

by Nangobi Bridget

Education

Education is important. Education is mother to this world.
School allows to achieve something in our future, when we work hard.
I was lucky to go to school, and was so excited on my first day. Then I started asking myself, who am I to be in this school?
I decide who I want to be in the future. My life will be the best. It is education that is useful.
Education is important.

by Nangobi Maria

The Young Women of Uganda

The young women of Uganda, they are their own future.
Their eyes have a special light.
It is the young women of Uganda who dress well for my classes
Who sit straight
With determination
And pride.

When classmates say that it is useless to educate a girl-child
They do not flinch or shout
But bow their heads and work a little harder.

They know the power of education
Their aspirations tower: I want to be a doctor, lawyer, nurse, physician,
I want to be an educator,
I want to end corruption in my country.

For the first time
I wear my womanhood with pride
To educate these girls
To be the hand
that helps them
to their greatness.

by Joanna Harker Shaw

Oh! The Book!

Oh! The book!
The book you can spend your time reading,
The book of all languages best for speaking,
The book that improve your writing and listening,
The wonderful book!

Oh! The book!
Is like a light to us,
Is like gold to me,
Is like my best friend to my life,
The wonderful book!

Oh! The book!
The book with good ideas
the book with poems and stories
The book with wisdom words to learn
The wonderful book!

Oh! The book
For the whole wide world,
For everyone to read,
For sharing and understanding,
The wonderful book!

by Kasadha Maliki Malson

## Books are Our Teachers

The book is a great helper,
With it I can learn prepositions,
with it I can learn homophones,
With it I can learn adverbs.
Books really are teachers.

The book is a great helper,
It gives me spellings,
It gives me definitions,
It gives me vocabulary.
Books really are teachers.

The book is a great helper,
If I am at home or at school,
It goes everywhere with me,
Everywhere I can learn.
Books are really teachers

The book is a great helper,
I can learn similes and poetry
I can learn proverbs
I can learn opposites and arguments
I can learn truth.
Books are really teachers.

*by Alibabwa Ali*

Song of a School Boy

Birds are singing in the forest
Waves are sparking in the river
All the leaves are all quivering
In the sunshine.

The clock's hands go on ticking
And the good lads go on learning
But I am yearning, simply yearning
For this lesson to be done.

When I am older and muscular
When I am at school no longer
When lesson times and student days
Are over

If there is a song in the forest
If the waves are sparkling on the river
fIf leaves are quivering
If the sun is shining
I will be out to greet them,
I will be out in the world


  by Katunde Abbay

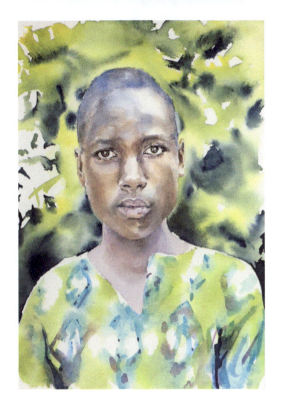

### Teaching from England

This magic window opens
Onto a morning
Six-thousand miles away
Where children
With all their anguish, hope, and wisdom, wait.
It is time for education
Theirs and mine.
Their dedication and determination
Their tiredness and impatience,
Their longing, all their longing,
For the beginning of the rest of their lives.

by Joanna Harker Shaw

## The Power of Words

Generations that have stood the test of time,
Foundations of the earth laid,
Rivers, lakes, oceans and seas,
Birds of air and animals of land
Created;
The utterance of a word.

Nations shaping their institutions
The Congress, House of Representative, Senate and Parliament,
Judicial systems thrive like bushfire
Prosperity of music and film
Cherishing the power of words.

Be students, teachers, politicians, scientists and authors,
We stitch words together
Relative to the confidence we have in them.
No doubt, the sky has always been the limit
In the efforts of our eloquence.

Zeal and Enthusiasm have taken their place,
Faith and Hope have prevailed.
Honesty, Diligence and Patriotism embodied
In the stories of our tales.
No amount of energy can take away
Your Word.

by Dhikusooka Ernest and Babirye Mary

## Nature

## Our Land

Land, land, land!
How wonderful you are!
On you we grow crops
Preventing famine,
On you forests grow
Helping the rainfall.

Weeds come from you
Which farmers use
To feed their animals.

Houses are our shelter,
Roads and railways
Constructed on your surface
Our transportation service.

Oh, Land, you are the source for all to our people!
This is why we research for you,
Day and night
Doing hard work

Mwesigwa Timothy

<u>Valley</u>

This is a low land,
a low land between two hills,
a land with good loam soil,
loam soils for good crops and good life.

A home to wild animals,
to the snakes and the frogs
to birds and crested cranes


by Kitimbo Viccent

## In Praise of the Flowers

Flower, Flower, Flower,
How good you are!
You help us in so many things,
You become our source of income
So we can buy what we need
to prosper in this tough world.

Flower, Flower, Flower,
How good you are!
The honey which is termed the sweetest,
Is made by the bees who are stealing
Your nectar,
Which you give so freely.

Flower, Flower, Flower
How good you are!
Sweet bright sunflowers
From which we make cooking oil
You are helping the entire world.

Flower, Flower, Flower,
How good you are!
We pick your colours and your scents
To decorate our ceremonies
Beautiful and perfumed
Weddings and parties.
Flower, Flower, Flower,
How good you are!

by Nangobi Maria

# Mountains

Mountains, the mountains
Mount Atlas, Mount Everest, Mount Moroto,
Mount Kenya, Mount Kilimanjaro
Mount Etna, Mount Speke, Mount Gessi,
Mountains more than tourist attractions.

Mountains, the mountains
Everywhere in the world.
All of different importance
And meaning.
Some are volcanoes
Some are black, some are white with snow
Or green with trees.
Some errupt with fire,
Some are the sources of water
All are important
A habitat for wild animals.

Mountains, the mountains,
Revered across the world.

by Kasule David (Rumumba)

## Protecting Our Forests

Landslides all over the world
Drought is a part of our climate
Famine and failing crops they say are unavoidable.

Blame none other than those
Who are cutting all the trees for fuel
Their actions lead to soil erosion
The landslides all over the world.

Keep the world green
Should be our motto,
For the greed of today
Will be the grief of tomorrow.

by Awino Maria

## From Seeds I Grow

From seeds I grow.
Taking years to mature,
Slow as a chameleon in growth.
You enjoy my fruits without feeding me.

From seeds I grow.
You rarely take care of me,
Greed and you are siblings.
You butcher me for timber,
yet you never helped my growth.

From seeds I grow.
I bring your rain,
I strengthen your soil,
You thank me by sawing my body
To burn it for charcoal.

See me, and feed me,
Spare my life for a better tomorrow...

by Kasadha Maliki Malson

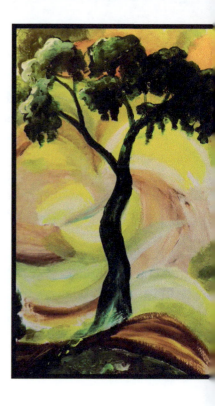

## The Tree

How useful I am!
I give you sweet fruits,
I purify the air,
I provide timber for your homes,
I am the tree!

I give you medicine for better health,
I give you firewood for food preparation,
I give homes to the tired birds,
And when the sunny season comes,
You can run to me for
I will give you shade.
I am the tree.

by Kintu Emmanuel

## The Sun's Song

I was created by God
To give man light
I am the sun shine
All through day time.

In the West I set;
In the East I rise.
At night you watch
For my morning skies.

All people smile when
They see my rays
All through the day
I bring happiness.

You tell me you love me,
I appreciate your love.
I am your light
And will light you forever.


by Mukisa Andrew

The Pearl of Africa

My mother land where the heart dwells
A land of untamed beauties
Hope and abundance hovers over her
Rich with the diversity of the African heritage
Many cultures, many races, many tribes
Basoda, Baganda, Banyankole, Langi, Acholi, Bunyoro
All of them pledging allegiance under one flag

The Nile River, Kiira, the Pride of the East
Cascading northwards across the vast land
From its source at Lake Victoria
A snow-capped mountain of the moon in the West
Its peak calmly kissing the clear blue sky
The dense Mabira tropical rainforest in the center
On the Eastern Edge is Mount Elgon
Covered with beautiful flora and fauna

A crested crane is a symbol of peace
Our flag: black, yellow, and red, all us count
Those in the country, and those in the cities
Young or old, able or disabled, rich or poor
We are the pearl of Africa

by Dhikusooka Ernest and Babirye Mary

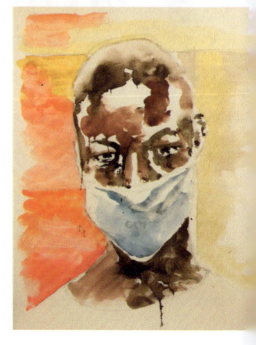

# Our Lives

## Walking with my Brothers

I was flying like the birds
For such inexpressible joy
As if was a dreaming

It was too long time
Like people waiting for their most lovers
To wash away stressing.

They are my light
Just like a bright future to me;
Amid the thunder, the lightening.

They keep me safe
From dangerous people ,
From kidnappers,
From defilement and neglect,
The dangers for a girl.
So I advise you my dear sisters
To walk with your brothers
And offer you a blessing.

by Nakisige Dorcus

<u>Little Mango</u>

My little mango,
You are the lucky seed
You are the lucky egg
My precious little mango.

My little mango,
In you I can see
A huge tall tree
Growing from a tiny seed.

My little mango
From you I see a ripe fruit
Hanging onto the branch
Sons and daughters and men
reaping

You my little one
Will sprout from the ground
Like a huge mahogany tree
And I'll rest in your shadow

Alibaawa Ali

## The Gift

Gifts Gifts Gifts
You are of a great value to us.
You help people express their love
For others.
Elder and youngsters
Be praised through you.
Gifts Gifts Gifts


You strengthen our love
During parties, ceremonies, birthdays.
Fathers and guardians use you to praise
The beloved, hard-working child.
Gifts Gifts Gifts
Gifts are kind like prayers
For orphans.
Gifts show our love.
Gifts Gifts Gifts

by Kintu Emmanuel

## My Queen

She
Is the good and nice looking girl
Shining like the dawn
Colourful like the rainbow
She is my queen.
Killing with scenic
feature on her body,
unique and exquisite girl.
I wish we become one person.

Oh! My queen, queen of beauty
I wish you last for centuries
Likable and never shaming,
Making me feel proud,
Girl of prestige,
Living so admirably.
You are part of my life.
My queen.

by Muwanguzi Samuel (Samuel Izon)

## Street Life! Street Life!

Life on the street is not easy.
We eat everything that could be called food,
Sometimes fine food from good hotels and markets.
Thank God for the Grand Imperial's leftovers!

Life on the street is tough.
Everything is hard to get.
Cold and rotten food is often our daily bread;
Birds, dogs, and wild things scramble for the cold, rotten food;
Ants and rats try their luck,
While we, the little ones, struggle,
Rubbish piles and dust bins are our hotels and markets.

Life on the street is harsh and rough.
Bare bodies are open to cold and heat,
Rainy and sunny skies are the same,
Cold when the sun has gone to sleep.
Now I will go back home, and I will say sorry.
I will leave this miserable life
On the street.

by Sebbide Kenneth

Poverty

Oh Poverty, I wander day and night,
Tracing your origins is all that is left,
Napless in the cold night.
I am looking for a silver penny
To get my son a book and a pen.
Indeed, Poverty, you are a fever.

You made her turn away for money,
Make her cheat and sulk,
Money for her baby's milk.
You are as cruel as death
Your orders broke her down.
On everyone's tongue is you, Poverty.

I hate you.
Your efforts show without fear
Can't hide that they are hurting.
They cut deeper and deeper and tear
And dangerously break a little heart
For sure they are sudden but they are clear.

No country, no city, no house is safe from you,
Over long distance you fly
I don't know why.
You do not spare our lives
Young and aged, beautiful and ugly

Beware of Poverty, you wealthy,
Perfectly fat, smooth and healthy.
*No worries*, they grin from ear to ear
Not caring if the orphans wear
To nothing, only care for those they bear.
How I hate you, oh, Poverty.

by Sebibbe Kenneth

## Building the Nation

Today I did my share
In building the nation.
I drove a permanent secretary
To an important, urgent function
In fact to a ceremonial luncheon.

The menu reflected its importance:
Cold beer with small talk,
Fried chicken with niceties,
Wine to fill the hollow laughs,
Ice-cream to cover the cruel jokes,
Coffees to keep the Secretary awake on return.

I drove the Permanent Secretary home.
He yawned many times in the back of the car
Then to keep awake he suddenly asked,
*Did you have any lunch, friend?*
I replied looking straight ahead
And secretly smiling at his belated concern,
That I had not, but was slimming!

Upon which he said with a seriousness
That amused more than annoyed me
*Mwananchi, I have eaten too much!*
*I attended to mattes of state*
*Delicate diplomatic duties, you know.*

*And friend, it goes against my grain,*
*Courses my stomach with ulcers and wind*
Ah, he continued, yawning again,
*The pains we suffer, building a nation.*

So the Permanent Secretary has ulcers too!
But are my ulcers more painful
From a certain hunger,

And not from sumptuous lunches!

So we each went home that evening
With terrible stomach pains.
The result of building the nation
In different ways.

by Nangobi Peace Praise

## Accidents! Accidents!

Worst thing in life!
You are as deadly as corona virus
You rob us of our dear ones
Sometimes large in numbers

We know what brings you:
Failure to follow highway codes
Speeding, drink-driving!
We do not learn,
And still you come.

You are common at cross-roads,
You are common at junctions,
You are common at roundabouts,
We know, but still you happen.

Shame on us, for we can stop you!
Accidents! Accidents!
Worst thing in life!


by Kasadha Maliki Malson

## Advice for the Children

CHILDREN CHILDREN
You are the hopes of every parent!
Whether rich or poor, young or old,
So you should work hard to make them
Happier in the world.
Hence, they will be proud of you.
Because of the future they
See in you
Always work hard.

CHILDREN CHILDREN
Your parents are putting their
investments in you
Waiting for profits.
Although sometimes losses
are seen,
Still, the investor
continue to invest in you.

CHILDREN CHILDREN
Make sure you take good
care.
After profits, boisterous fruits
are herded
A bright, successful future
For both your people
and yourself.

Always work hard.

by Kintu Emmanuel

## Always Read Good News

Good news, good news,
The news here and there
The news in and out
The minister is coming

The good news spread
The good news reached everywhere
Happiness felt
The minister is coming.

The media gave us good news
The radio gave us good news
The televeision gave us good news
The minister is coming

Like a thief the day came
Like a their it happened
The reporters reported
The minister is coming
Because of good news I went
I went to see the minister.

By Kasadha Malson Maliki

## A Mother's Song

I have never seen a man like my husband
Very lazy and meaningless
Highly qualified with a masters degree
But too lazy to find a job
Don't be like your father, son.

He never goes to the garden
He says dirty work is for illiterates
Like me your mother
My husband drinks a lot and starves the family;
Don't be like your father, son.

My husband is handsome but meaningless
too lazy to graze the cattle, sheep and goats
He is weak and careless to repair the kitchen,
The local brew is his only business.
Don't be like your father, son.

He is not responsible at all
My heart is wounded and my back broken,
Because i perform his responsibilities
To keep the family going.
Don't be like your father, son,
when you grow up.

Sebidde Kennth
*of Uganda, the Pearl of Africa*

Sponsors

Sponsors are good.
And I can tell much about them.
Haven't you heard?
They are bees pollinating flowers to get nectar
And so the flowering plant is helped to bear fruits.
As I speak I was once sponsored by a lady called Patience
Who paid my fees for my primary seven.

Sponsors, sponsors, sponsors!

You are the loving bees which can easily be attracted by little flowers,
Hence helping them become fantastic plants that bear
Marvellous kind of fruits which are useful to the world!
This is our unity.

I can conclude by saying that sponsors are good people
Such people deserve to be happy.

by Mukisa Andrew

## The Good of my Sister

In terrible and good conditions
I look forward to her

On her being small, poor but
religious she provides her best

She fails sometimes but not
from inside her heart top.


by Muwanguzi Samuel (Samuel Izon)

# The World

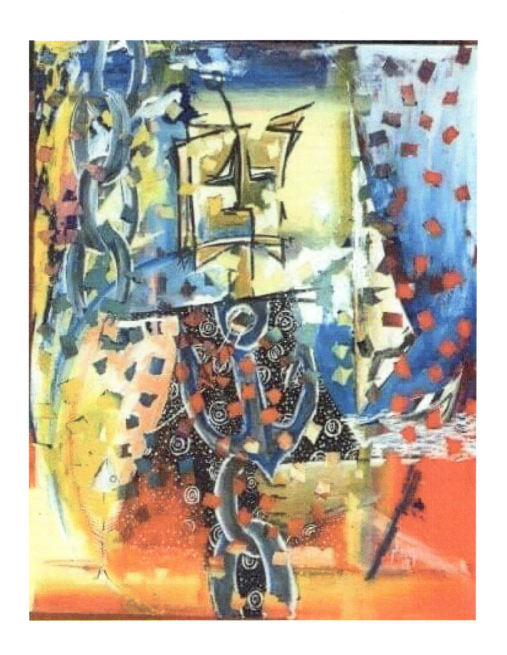

## Life Life Life!

I am Life and I am good
People love me, because all life is good.
I am Life, I am Life!

I am Life and I am good
All are my family, and I give to all.
Enjoy every moment for I am so good.
I am life! I am Life!
Life is the best!

Nangobi Bridget

## Death

Yes, it is true,
I do make sure to serve the world.
No one will live any longer than I say.
Yes, I am certain and real.

I could catch you when you are old or twenty.
This day or next day, I am ready.
What advice I give is to pursue daily,
Your strength and health
And keep me waiting.

by Mukyane Faruku

## Time

Time is
Mine and yours
Sixty seconds put together
Makes a minute

Then hours, weeks and months
Then a year
You and I grow, end comes near
Time, then we die

Things change but not her
All things die
Except time.

by Kintu Emmanuel

## The Grace

To live a happy life we need grace.
Helping those in need
We lead and others follow
How good is grace?


Living in a peaceful world
We have to forgive one another
Only grace makes kith
How good is grace?

Grace creates humbleness
Reconciling friends
Everyone can have the grace
How good is grace?

by Mukisa Andrew

Diseases

Oh, disease!
Small in size, but painful.
Caused so easily,
So easily transmitted.
Oh, disease!
Such a dangerous thing
It spares nobody.
Attacks the children and the mature,
officers, doctors, rich and poor
How shall we survive this?
Together we can!
Let us stand
Together to fight the enemy!
Together wash away disease
Together do what the doctors say.
Oh, disease!
Together we can survive.


by Kitamirike Deogratius

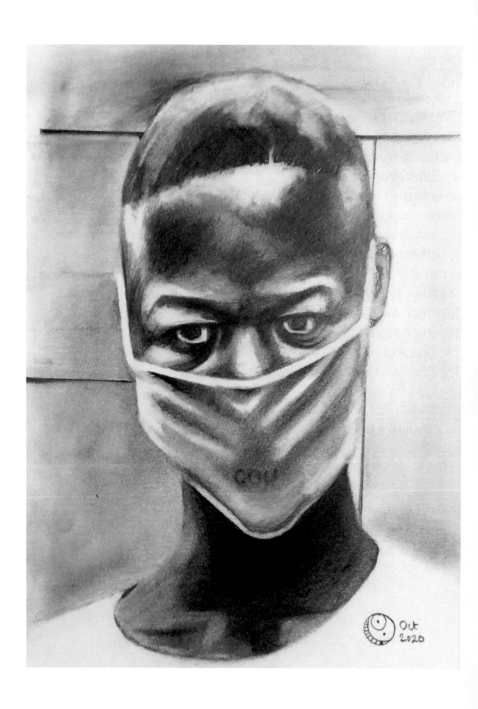

## COVID-19

Unknowingly, I became a disturbing disease,
A pandemic across the world I spread.
I still spread
Oh! I am very dangerous.

I am tiny but destructive.
In unique ways researchers understood
Me not only as a virus but even
The symptoms I leave after attack
Aches, pains, fever, cough.
Oh! I am very dangerous.

However, I have put the world at lock
Scientists fight much to stop me,
by putting their preventive measures.
Religious people look to the lord,
In order to stop and destroy me
Yet still, I remain so dangerous.

by Muwanguzi Samuel (Samuel Izon)

## A Future Without Trees

Imagine
Imagine a treeless world, one so bare
An era where open green became so rare
Imagine a time when there is an earth to share
Will we be safe? Will it be fair?

Imagine an earth where forests are no more
Will we survive? Will they glamour?
The scorching sun, the peeling skin
Will we survive? Will they blossom?
A world of carbon monoxide gas
Will we survive? Will they respire?

A wasted world withered in stature
A desolated earth devoid of nature
The masterpiece of our reckless designs
If the relentless deforester never resigns

If only we stood firm in the resolution
To preserve our trees from gruesome extinction
If only we considered this as the ultiamte solution
Then we will survive a tragic annihilation
Plant a tree, save the future is our proclamation.

by Dhikusooka Ernest

## Fire Bird

May the mighty God bless you
Fire Bird, it seems that you are very wise
They trained you but
How wrong you were to accept a lone master.
You have been named the fire bird because you burn
Or so it seems like when you are in flight,
Yet you are useful to us too,
Carrying flower pollen seeds
May the mighty God bless you
Such that you live longer than the rest,
Fire bird, we cannot even start to celebrate your beauty!
May the mighty God bless you, fire bird.

by Mukyawe Faruku

## Learning In Lockdown

In what feels like the end of days
Where we hide in our shelters
We keep up the widest space
Around our fragile selves

We cannot connect by touch
We cannot embrace in love
We cannot pursue our dreams
Or travel too far

Yet, a lifeline
In strange new places
A thought we hadn't considered
Begins to grow.
We reach out
In new ways
These days are new days
Computers become
Our windows onto the world.

We find such amazing things
When we consider what could be
And send out our words
To touch someone new.

By Joanna Harker Shaw

# About The Artists

*This book owes a great debt to the artists who permitted the reproductions of their work free of charge. All of the portraits in this book are portraits of the poets and fellow students of the Busano Community.*

### EmmaLou Andrews
Working mostly in pencil, I work hard to create art that evokes joy and memories in people. I'm passionate to evolve as an artist, exploring more themes and subjects as art comes naturally to me, relaxes me and makes me happy.
Facebook.com/emmalouartist

### Nadine Bailey
Nadine Bailey is cross-media portrait artist based in London, England, whose work aims to capture an engaging impression of the character of her sitter and build a connection with the viewer. She regularly posts her latest portraits on her Instagram @luxnax and website nadinebailey.myportfolio.com

### Ian Dawber FSIAD
A Designer, Illustrator and Artist based in the North West of England, Ian is an elected member of the Society of Illustrators, Artists and Designers, a member of The Royal Glasgow Institute of the Fine Arts and has taken part in art exhibitions in

Glasgow, Manchester, Stockport, Nottingham, Warrington and his home town Wigan.

### Karen Gould

I was born and live in England. I am married and come from a large family. Have always loved drawing since I could hold a pencil and enjoy the variety of working in all art mediums.
My artwork can be found on Facebook, Instagram and Twitter
https://www.facebook.com/KGTimeForArt/
Instagram.com/kgtimeforart

### Joanna Harker Shaw

Although principally a poet, editor Jo has illustrated several of her poetry books including *Songs of the River* and *The Witches of Aira Falls*. It has been a particular pleasure for her to draw her students for this book.

### Margaret Harker

Margaret Harker is a writer, artist and musician. She currently lives in Cumbria where the beautiful landscape inspires her to create her oil landscape paintings.

### Dominic Hendow Hendy

Dominic Hendy is a Cornish artist based in Brighton. Primarily working with drawing and painting, Hendy often contrasts dark subject matter with the use of vivid colours, provoking intense emotional reactions. His painterly technique gives the

impression of the subject matter in motion, allowing the viewer to gain a stronger connection to the work.
Instagram- @dom.tzr

## Simon Humphreys

Simon Humphreys is an artist who has lived in Strathearn, Scotland with his family for many years. He enjoys producing bold portraits of bold folk and has no doubt this comes from a 25 year career in social care, working with people when at their most dynamic, inspiring and vulnerable. More of Simon's work can be found at facebook.com/pdmportraits and
instagram.com/pdm_portraits

## Lucas Kumba

Lucas Khumba is a South African artist of Congolese descent, born in 1995. He completed his high school studies at New Nation School, Johannesburg. Lucas joined the Little Artists School Project in 2007, whilst he was still in primary school, over the years he received lynd Price Webber Wentzel, most hard working artist, highly commanded Webber Wentzel. Lucas furthered his studied at Artist Proof Studio in professional printmaking.

He has exhibited at Graham Gallery, Johannesburg Stock Exchange, Deutsche Bank, Marry Edwards House, Absa and Khayalami.

Lucas currently is a full time artists and volunteers at Little Artists School Project.

## Mayank Manna

Mayanak Manna is an exceedingly talented junior artist (13 years old) from Haldia, West Bengal, India. 'I pass my pleasure time by sketching and playing with colours. I try to express my little feelings on canvas.

I want a space in people's heart as a great artist. I want your blessings only. Thank you.' https://www.facebook.com/mannamayank/

Susan Mansi

"Painting came to me under its own steam. Somewhere in the struggle between words and images I started to make images. It's a different enterprise to writing. Both ask for precision but the eye has a different response to precision than the ear does. I love colour, form, texture, image, story, development, materials, and the surprise thing that happens when I surrender to it all."

Angela Ortenzi-MacColl

I'm Angela Ortenzi-MacColl of Art Decoup-Ange. I'm a mixed media artist of non traditional decoupage works, born from a love of textiles and patterns. I returned to Art less than a year ago, 23 yrs after graduating with BA in Fine Art. My work is figurative, highly decorative and intricate. I aim for a lighthearted look at my character, humour, self image and emotions to connect with others who feel they're just bumbling through this life!
http:www.facebook.com/artdecoupange/

Nana Osei

Nana Osei( Victor Osei Mensah) is a self taught artist born in the Central region of Ghana and brought up in the

capital city Accra. As an expressionist, semi-abstract artist working in terracotta and acrylic, subjects are mostly imaginary human figures depicting emotions which are not easily noticed. Acrylics on canvas is the main medium for his paintings and life on earth as his personal inspiration. He is inspired by experiences of life on earth and the society as it evolves. He believes every form of art is beautiful.

## Jayne Perkins

Jayne Perkins is a primary school teacher and mum-of-two who runs facebook.com/Kinsperart

"I am a self-taught artist and learn through trying different styles. I love bold outlines and mixing media and painting particularly natural world and wildlife subjects and scenes."

## Kerry Whiteley

My love of watercolours and the wonderfully unexpected nature of the medium started 20 years ago. Since joining an online watercolour group I have focused more on portrait realism, working principally from photographs, exploring the strong light and shadow contrasts.

My paintings can be viewed on Facebook and Instagram @kerryW_art

# Busano Community Initiative Uganda (BCIU) ]

Nkaaba Jude and Joanna Harker Shaw begin the Saturday morning English class via videocall.

Students gather outside on a sunny day for class.
Front row: Nangobi Immaculate, Nankwalu Saida, Kiroko Rigan
Middle row: Nangobi Maria, Banalaya Joseph, Mwesigwa Timothy
Back row: Kalume Ibrahim, Katudde Abbay
Standing: teaching assistant Babiyre Mary

L-R Mukisa Samuel, Nangobi Bridget, Kasadha Malson Maliki, Nangobi Peace Praise, Sebidde Fahad, Nkisige Dorcus, Alibawa Ali, Mukisa Andrew and Mukyawe Farouk.

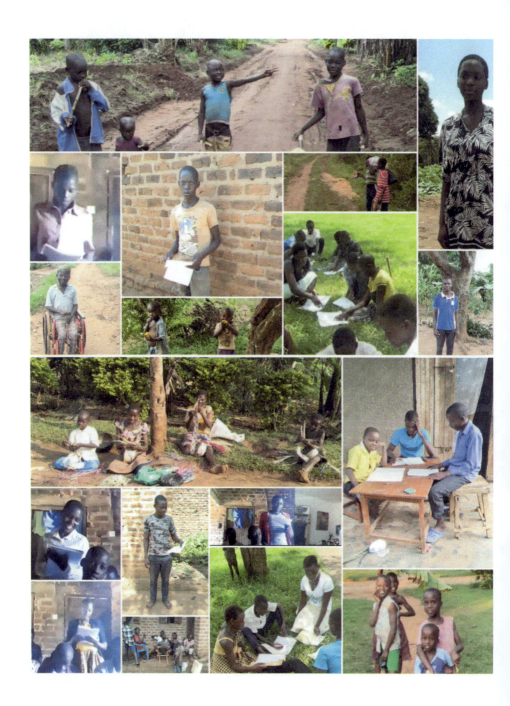

Busano Community Initiative Uganda is an NGO located in the Kamuli district. Their objective is to improve the conditions of the local community through education and vocational training.

I encourage you to read about their work on their website
https://busano-uganda.jimdosite.com/

There you can find out information about the work they are doing, find details of the students who are seeking penpals (many of whom have work featured in this book), and learn how you can send support.

I hope you have enjoyed this book.

                            Jo Harker Shaw